Inherit the Dawn

P.Bodi

Let it light you up slow,
Let it take its time,
Don't rush hope,
Trust that it will
Arrive.

To be afraid is to be human,
To be brave is human too,
You build strength in doing
What you're scared to do.

Deciding to recover
Is an act of courage,
The dedication to
Grow, to flourish.

Make your mental health a
Priority, choose to put energy
To growth,

Of self-hate and self-forgiveness,
You cannot have both.

'Brave' looks like you, holding
Onto another day—another
Morning met,

Breathing light, taking
It in, to every next
Sunset.

You are not your suffering,
While it is real, and it matters,
You don't end there,

There is more of you to find,
There is more of you to share.

We need reminders sometimes
For why we try our best, why
We give ourselves our best,

And on our journey, on our way,
We do our best not to forget.

This is hard work—
Walking into the unknown,
The quiet dark of a path
You've never taken,

Trust that day will come,
This getting better comes
With courage as well
As patience.

Does the flower ask
The sun if it can bloom?
 No, and neither should
You, you are not a
Burden or to blame
For your pain, and
Asking for help does
Not deserve your shame.

Do what it takes to survive,
The small things can keep
Us going, don't fault yourself
For the rate at which
You're growing.

Asking for help, being
Open, is not attention
Seeking—don't let
Anyone convince you
That reaching out can't
Be the beginning of
Your healing.

You are not your illness,
Not your trauma, wounds,
Or hurt,

You are not
Defined by the pain
In your mind, you are
Illness second,
Human first.

Be the person you needed
When you were at your lowest,
When you needed someone to
Be there to say it'll all be okay—
That it's okay to not be okay,

That you are more than your shame,
That others feel the same way.

You are strong,
On both the days
You can't get up,
And those that
You do,

Be proud of staying,
Of being here now,
And have empathy
For the struggle, too.

If you have been hurt,
That means you have
Seen more of the human
Experience—you, human,

Despite it all, you are
Glowing, you are blooming.

We all fall,
Heavy from the sky,
Falling harder for the
Way we have risen,

This too is a part
Of the process,
This too is living.

Discomfort is a natural part of change,
Like how the night squints its eyes at the
Sun until it has blossomed into day,
The heavy and the cold lifted into
Morning's light,

Dawn's warmth is worth the fight.

Rest is an essential
Part of your journey,
Recovery is not
Something to
Be hurried,

Have compassion,
Empathy, and give
Yourself grace, this
Life is not a race.

Every day,
You are growing
Into the best
Version of yourself,
The best 'you' the
World has seen—

Treasure too, every
'You' there is,
In the in-between.

You are not a burden,
Mental illness is not
A death sentence,
There is life beyond
A diagnosis,

You are more than
Your lowest moments.

Negativity cannot
Be questioned if
It's kept inside
And on its
Own,

We cannot change
That which we
Leave alone.

I know you, I see you,
I've been there the same,

Thinking it'd never get
Better—this invisible pain,

But the mind is a trainable
Thing I've come to know,

Every day, with effort,
You can continue to grow.

Mental illness was
Not a choice you've
Made, this isn't your
Fault, not a decision,

Even then, even still,
It's up to us to live, to rise
From what we've been
Given.

Wounds that can't be seen,
The deep cuts that are hard
To explain,

They deserve to be healed,
And they don't deserve your shame.

Be the support you need,
Find comfort in 'alone'
Instead of fear, and be kind
When you need it most,

Sometimes we're the
Only ones we can
Keep close.

Courage, this is courage,
Living, breathing, existing,
Despite all that you've
Experienced and what
You've been through,

Be proud, because this
Strength is profound,
And remember that
It's all found in you.

Asking for what you need
Gives others the permission
To do the same,

It challenges silence,
And it challenges shame.

Doubt is natural when nothing
Has helped for so long,

The fact that you're still trying,
Still here now—that is what
It means to be strong.

Nothing left to lose,
Or so you may feel,
Sunk to rock bottom,

But you still have yourself,
You still have a future
To make, you are not
Less for having fallen.

Treatment is not
A smooth line from
Illness to recovery,

But we get closer
With every new
Lesson learned,
With every new
Discovery.

You are not unlovable
For your mental illness,
Not loved 'despite',
You are loved for all
That you are, the dark
As well as the light.

You matter,
Even when
You're convinced
That you don't,

Self-belief will not
Always be an unknown.

Hope is hard to hold with
Unsteady hands, shaking
Fingers—uncertain and
Afraid,

Thinking, 'What if I'm hurt
Again, what if I lose hope
Just the same?'

But hope can grow,
And hope can stay,
In the face of all
That's dark and
Gray.

Relapse, falling back,
Sinking to the familiar lows,
Even then, even here,
That is part of your growth,

Recovery has no
Place for perfection,
And you can re-frame
Your missteps as a lesson.

Purpose isn't easily found,
Exploration is required,
Keep searching for
That thing that'll
Keep you warm,
Alight, inspired.

Believe me now if you
Won't believe in yourself:
You have the capacity
To grow,

Let yourself stay until
This is a truth that you know.

No one gets prizes, medals,
Ribbons for their suffering,
You are not any less worthy
Of help than someone that
Seems to have it 'worse',
The only reward you can
Give yourself is recovering,
To recognize that you
Are valid in your hurt.

Loving yourself is not
A destination, it is a work
In progress, and lapsing
Into old ways of thinking
Is a practice in forgiving.

Your voice matters,
Let yourself be
Loud and clear,

Your story deserves
To be told, and there is
A place for you here.

'Dead-ends'? There are none.
Change comes in many forms—
Never done, we can't assume
Our journey is over, knowing now
What doesn't work just brings
Recovery closer,

Trial and error takes time,
Effort, and heart, every
Day is its own new start.

There is the unexpected
In your future, the 'Not
Yet known', the surprises
That will challenge your
Harsh expectations—

Your self fulfilling
Prophecies are
Not truth, but its
Convincing
Imitation.

Being yourself, stepping into
The certainty that you are
Who you are, lets others
See that they don't have to hide,

What a gift, to be
Another's guide.

Your pain is valid,
Leave comparisons
Behind,

Don't let it stop you
From getting help,
Don't let your struggle
Be denied.

Everything counts,
Every step you take—
The little as important
As the large,

Trying, in earnest, and
Doing your best will
Take you far.

Not a burden,
Not undeserving,
Not broken, not
A mess to be
Cleaned up,

You are so
Endlessly
Enough.

Even though it hurts to feel,
Pain's presence needs its
Time to heal,

Moments will come and pass
In the way that they will, there
Is patience in the word 'until'.

So maybe you've
Been struggling
Again,

Maybe it's all
Pulling at your
Edges—the dark,
The cold, the heavy,

But this getting better
Doesn't look one way,
Doesn't feel one way,
Because that too
Is recovery,

It's a sign to keep on
Going—coping with
That pain is a part
Of growing.

Before,
Before,
And now,
In after,

But a diagnosis
Does not mean
Disaster,

You have awareness now,
The capacity to choose,

Give yourself the effort
That will bring you
Closer back to you.

Who were you,
That you're not
Now?

Who are
You in this
Moment?

Embrace the 'you' in
Moments past, and the
'You' that you are growing.

It's in the rise and fall
Of each breath,
The present moment
Never leaves,

Opening yourself to the
Here, the now, can bring
A sense of calm, relief,

The mind flutters, jumps,
From the future to the past,
Find yourself as you are,
Where the mind can
Rest at last.

Do not invalidate yourself,
As hard as it may be, especially
When others have contributed
To those feelings, that shame,

Know that your struggle is real,
And you are not to blame for
Feeling this way,
No matter what
Others may say.

Maybe you feel out of place,
Like a stranger among
Family and friends,
Perhaps you feel like an
Imposter, like you always
Have to pretend,

And there's something
Magic in showing up
Just as you are,
Just as you come—
Flaws and worries and
Strengths and humor,
The capacity to love and
Be loved—and if you keep
Trying to connect, that
Is in your future.

Don't share until you're ready,
But know that when you do—
You're helping break the stigma,
Mend the shame for others as
Well as for you.

Believing in your recovery,
Or rejecting the chance to
Flourish, trying in earnest,
And getting discouraged,

Do your best in every moment,
Because that's the only thing
You can do, find things that
You find motivating, because
Recovery's in you.

This fight is worth it,
You are worth it,
Even when you
Don't believe it,

We must keep going—
We can keep growing,
Despite the defeat
We may be feeling.

Everyone is going through
Something—yet still
We pass judgment,

You never really know
Another's struggle, and
Sometimes we keep
It all inside,

But we're all less
Different than we
Are alike.

Confidence is not arrogance,
Self-love is not greedy and
Does not deserve your
Guilt, or your shame,

Self-respect and narcissism
Are not the same.

An emptiness,
A numbness,
A nothingness,
An absence,

Loss of pleasure,
Purpose, passion,

A present muted, drawn gray,
Is still not a promise that
Life will always be
The same way.

Courage is you
Staying another day
Despite all that's happened,

Give yourself kindness,
Give yourself compassion.

Inherit the Dawn

Frantic, desperate, or still and numb,
Searching for a cure, for help, relief,
Can feel like nothing is ever enough,

We walk through the black,
Arms stretched out to find a light,
When all we get is empty space,
It can feel like this isn't
Worth the fight,

But you are not running out of time,
And hopelessness wants to see you
Stay in that dark—but it is not a
Sign that it will last forever,

Continuing to search, to reach,
To push forward,
Will send you on the path
To getting better.

The people who would be
Happy if you weren't around
Aren't worth keeping close,

Surround yourself with
Those who want to see
Your growth.

You are valid,
Your struggle
Is worthy of help
No matter what,

You are deserving,
You are enough.

Idle, idealizing,
'Anywhere but here',
Not every moment is a
Moment we want to stay in,
Sunk in paralyzing fear,

But there's something magic
In the moments we let be
And nothing more,

No expectation, just the rhythm,
Like the heartbeat of the shore.

You matter,
You matter,
Just the same
As any other
Person,

You are deserving
Of love, of worth,
And you are not
A burden just
Because you're
Hurting.

Imagine, what would you
Do if you had no fear?
Would you do that thing
You've been avoiding,
Say what has been
Waiting to be said,
Be the person you've
Wanted to be all along?

You may not be there yet,
But you can learn to shift
The way you respond.

Living is not a simple thing,
When you've simply not
Wanted to be,

When tomorrow was
Unthinkable, when 'today'
Was a place you've wanted
To leave,

You've touched pain,
And maybe you
Haven't yet met
The light,

Give yourself the
Chance for things
To change, because
You are worth
The fight.

Respect yourself,
Don't say 'sorry' for
What doesn't deserve
An apology or your
Shame,

Sincerity and
Self-deprecation
Are not the same.

Breathe,
There is space
Between one
Moment and
The next,

Waiting just
For you—
Waiting all
Along,

Just like how the
Night is patient
For the dawn.

They're just lines your
Brain has rehearsed—
Not gospel, not a reflection
Of anything true,

You can talk back to
Fear, to what feels
Convincing and real,
There is more to you.

Slipping does not
Erase what you've
Achieved,

Missteps do not
Mean defeat.

Find that thing that
Lights you up—
That gets to the
Heart of it all,
That touches
You to your core,

That makes you feel
More yourself,
That thing that you
Can call yours.

Self-destruction,
We have struck the
Match that lit the fuse,

Thinking—
'If I never really
Try in the first place,
There's no way that I
Can lose',

But we have to give
Ourselves more of a
Chance to succeed,

Instead of letting
Failure be our
Guarantee.

Mental illness is not a choice—
No one would struggle if
That were true,

There'd be no blame, no
Stigma, if they suffered
The way we do.

Believe what you will,
But I see it in you still—
You've got that fight,
That tooth and claw,

To beat what holds you down,
To get back up after every fall.

Things end,
And we sometimes
Never get the closure
We feel we need,

How to heal the wounds
That no one else can see?

But your hurt is important,
Your loss matters,
There is still beauty to be
Known in your 'after'.

Your sensitivity is not a flaw,
Showing your emotions
Is not weakness, but a
Source of connection—
Touching the pulse of
What it means to be
A person,

There is depth, there is growth,
In your highs, in your lows,
In your joy and in your hurting.

It passes, it does.
It all passes,
It goes just the
Same way that
It comes.

We can feel trapped
In our feelings,
Hostage to highs and
Lows we didn't ask for,
Desperate to get out,
Get them gone,

It's hard to recognize they're
All necessary ways to be,
That this is the way through,
That we're not lost.

It's worth it in the end,
And that's easy to
Forget, easy to deny,

You are worth
Feeling better,
And you have the
Strength to try.

Happiness is not a
Choice we can make,
Not something we
Can fake—

No, we cannot tell
Ourselves what to feel,
Sometimes we just
Have to be honest,
To be unapologetically real.

Anxiety is a liar,
The devil on
Your shoulder,
Telling you all
The things you
Fear will come
True,

But you have the
Power to question
That which fear
Assumes.

Child you once were,
Before the mask that
We all learned,

Connect to what you
Wanted at your purest,
Touch the glow you've
Had in you from the
Beginning,

Bring to light the
Treasures 'Growing
Up' has hidden.

It's ok to feel uncomfortable,
Angry, sad, lonely—they are
All necessary emotions,

Try and stay open to them,
Even in your hardest moments,

Don't ignore, push down, or deny,
Let yourself feel it all,
It's okay to break down,
To get upset, to cry.

Your mental illness is not your fault,
And shame is a thousand quiet deaths,

Yet there you are,
A light in the dark,
Taking it breath by breath.

Falls can teach us
If we let them,
We're not broken
Just for struggling,

Perfection has no
Place in recovering.

Hopelessness can
Pass the same as any
Other feeling,

It too can exist
In the pursuit of healing.

Built up just to
Break back down,
Or so it seems,
But falling doesn't erase
All that you've achieved,

You can stand up,
Rise against,
Push forward,
Again and again.

Bring your wounds,
Your worries, lay them
Down and look at
Them close—

What part of them holds
A lesson to learn,
What part of them holds hope?

Your journey is your own,
And your comparisons
Do not help you get
To where you want
To be in this life,

You will grow as
Only you can,
In your own way,
In your own time.

Give someone else
What you may want—
An unconditional
Sort of kindness,
The kind that waits,

Because even if
You're not where
You want to be,

You have everything
It takes.

Light at the end of the tunnel,
Tunnel vision, but there isn't
Just one track to take,
No single way forward,
And there's no end point
At which to rest,

You can forge your own path,
And reaching into the unknown
Is its own success.

We hold hands with the things
That scare us, maybe tighter
Than with the things we desire,
Passion can slip too easy, and
Fear can be a divider,

How to reach, to try and grow,
When we stop ourselves before
We begin,

Only when I talked back to
Terror could I truly start to live.

Sometimes we get so
Tired, how to keep
Going when all we
Want to do is let go?

Don't forget you can rest,
Take pause—this too
Is a part of our growth.

How would you treat
Yourself differently
If you truly felt you
Were deserving?

Sure of your worth,
No longer uncertain,

Self-respect is a practice,
It takes time to make it
Feel true,

It is within your reach,
Within the actions
You can take,
A challenge you
Can choose.

Depression is exhausting,
Heavy body struggling to
Get out of bed,
To not have a good day,
But a 'day' at all,

Even then we can break the
Big steps down to parts,
There is no effort
Too small.

When you've lived with
Mental illness all your life,
There is no 'before' to
Guide the way,

It's even harder to build the
Trust that it will improve
At all one day,

Hope is hard to harness,
How to hold onto a light
You've never known?

This is when it's most
Essential to let yourself
And others remind you,
That getting better is still
Possible, that even here,
Your hope can be grown.

I've lost sight of myself,
The 'me' somewhere up ahead,
The one that knows
What's best, what's true,

We get side-tracked,
But we've always known
What to do,

Take the next step,
Then another,
And keep yourself
In mind,

What do you want
For yourself, truly,
What do you want,
At your most kind?

We are reflected in
Every person
That we touch,
Like ripples from
A stones throw,

This is a way we make meaning,
To watch not just ourselves,
But others grow.

Pressure, stressors,
Anxiety and overwhelm,

Sometimes our biggest
Obstacle is ourselves,

Breathe and breathe and breathe,
You are enough, you are here,
And you are more than your fear.

It takes time,
Give yourself time,
Patience as your
Guide,

We cannot rush
That which must
Be grown—let yourself
Flourish into the unknown.

Prioritize yourself,
Don't become the
Bearer of everyone
Else's bad news,

And you can't truly
Be there for others
If you don't take
Care of you,

Supporting others is a virtue,
But remember to take
Time for yourself,

You deserve your own love,
You deserve your own help.

There is purpose,
There is meaning,
For only you to make,

Hold excitement, hope,
For all that you'll create.

Your future is not determined,
So try to be determined
To treat yourself with care,
With kindness, with love,

We spend the most time with ourselves,
We must be the ones to remind
Ourselves that we are enough.

Maybe the hard times,
The dark heavy days
Have returned,
Despite all the
Work you've done,
After all the progress
You've made,

Remember,
No matter how distressing,
That is not a guarantee that
Those days are here to stay.

Don't let others tell you
It's a personal failing,
Because it's not,
They're wrong,

No one would choose an
Illness, to suffer this way,
No, this isn't your fault.

Your pain is not something
You have to apologize for,
And sharing it is not a mistake,

There are those that
Want to hear it all,
And there are those
That can relate.

You were not made to entertain—
To ignore your wants and needs
For others benefit,

Your life is not a show or a performance,
Your feelings aren't irrelevant.

Reflect on your surroundings
And the people you keep close,
Do they cut the stems that reach,
Do they crush the buds that grow?

Let yourself be choosey,
Find the ones that want your best,
Find the ones that make you more,
Not the ones that make you less.

It's an itch—
The desire to
Do our worst,

Self-destruction,
Self-sabotage,
Committed to
Our hurt,

It feels bittersweet,
But it's only bitter
In the end,

What if we
Chose to be kind,
Kind to our body,
Kind to our mind,
Kind to others instead?

Some days,
Getting up,
Being a person,
Is harder than
In days past,

It leaves me afraid,
That my better days
Won't last,

But I can't tell the future,
Even though hopelessness
Likes to try,

Even if it doesn't feel like
It in the moment,
Even then, I'll be alright.

No cure is ever sure,
No guarantee to be
Guaranteed,

And sometimes we
Don't get the things
We really need,

But still we rise,
Like a new day's sun,
As bright as we can be,
There's something
Magic in the start
Of self-belief.

When we feel less human,
And more of an illness,
When we feel
Alone and
Low,

That just means you
Have even more room
To grow.

'It will pass' has never
Resonated with me,
It never felt true—
Not when it comes back again,
Dark times not an 'if' but a when,
No matter what I'd do,

But this is what I have learned:
Surviving is its own success,
You can't help but change everyday,
And all you can do is do your best.

There is nothing final in the
Journey to becoming well,
It is a constant upkeep to
Maintain your mental health,

This is not discouragement,
But acknowledgment of
How proud you should be
For fighting each day,
For not letting mental
Illness have its way.

I've thought something was wrong
With me, felt down deep inside,
Leaving me uneasy with that
Constant question 'why?',

But I don't have an answer,
And I don't think it's worth my time,
Sometimes feelings don't make sense—
They don't always need to be defined.

Do not compare your
Journey with others,
I have found it to
Be suffering upon
Suffering,

A punishment
For not being where
I thought I 'should' be,
Where I saw others thriving—
I was doing all I could just
To keep surviving,

But we all move at
A different pace,
We all have our strengths
And limitations,

Try and be only the best
Version of you, not someone
Else's imitation.

Don't ignore yourself,
Awareness is the first
Step to finding help.

I was sure nothing would ever help,
So sure that I worked to dig my own grave,
Self-sabotage an old friend,

Despite what I believed,
None of my attempts at getting better
Were dead-ends,

There was more for me to do,
There is more out there for you, too.

You are whole,
With or without
Others at your
Side,

Being alone doesn't
Mean you can't thrive.

Feeling is not fact,
We see things not as
They are, but as we are—
And our fears and lows
Are liars, they can't
Always be trusted,

How much time do we
Spend standing still on
All the "What-if's"?

In your worst moments—
Yes, worst; the moments
You're scared to feel again,
The moments you never
Want to feel again,

Caught in the suspense
Of 'when, when, when
Will it end?'

Sometimes we don't get
Relief when we need it,
When we feel our most defeated,

If nothing more,
Give yourself a reason—
Give yourself, small or no,
A reason to keep on breathing.

You are not responsible
For others emotions—
Growing up, I thought it was
My responsibility to help
Others feel good,

I forgot myself in the end,
Too concerned with everyone
Else to be understood,

But now, I tend to my
Own well-being—
A kindness, a freedom,

Self-love something I believe in.

There is no perfection in this world,
And if you are holding yourself
To that impossible standard,
You'll feel unfulfilled—
It only ends one way,

Try your best not to give
Perfectionism its say.

How do we manage the anxiety,
The sadness, the numbness,
When we're right in the middle
Of it all, feeling paralyzed?

It's hard to recognize it
In the moment, nearly
Impossible, that this
Too we will survive.

Let yourself be proud
Of the small things,
Anything you find
Hard to do is worth
Acknowledging,

Even if it may not be a
Struggle for others—
Your path is the only
One you need to
Be following.

You, burden?
No, you are human,
Doing the best with
What you've got,

Do all that you have
The capacity to do,
Moment to moment,
And forgive what
You cannot.

Blaming the bad on ourselves,
And the good on anything else,
We don't give ourselves enough
Credit or enough slack,

Progress comes when
We have our own back.

If you want to be heard,
Be direct—honesty,
Vulnerability, is how
We best connect.

What mask have you
Been taught to wear,
With words that you've
Been made to speak?

What have you been
Convinced to hide,
That which makes
You unique?

We can unlearn these
Faces, these words,
These ways of living
In quiet hurt.

Do not let anyone shame you
Into pretending you are fine,
Your feelings aren't up to
Them to decide.

Be kind to yourself,
In those moments where
You are nowhere near
Where you want to be,
Pressure will not let
Things fall into place,

You are not being timed,
And life is not a race.

Sometimes you have
To sit in the anxiety,
Avoidance may have
Led you to isolation,

Fears compound
When left alone,
And sometimes we have
To give ourselves the
Invitation to face them,
To be afraid, to grow.

Resting is essential,
Pushing yourself is too,
You need both if you
Want to improve.

The experience of suffering
Is different for everyone,
And mental illness does
Not have a look,

Just because we're
Diagnosed the same,
Doesn't mean I've stood
Where you've stood.

Feelings don't always connect,
And that doesn't make you less
Of a person, or unworthy of love,

Rejection doesn't mean you're
Not enough.

You've survived your
Darkest days if you
Are here now to
Read this poem,

I see you,
I've been you,
Feeling lost and at
Your lowest,

But you can be found—
There are others all around,
Those who have felt the same way,

Let yourself meet
Them where you are,
Let yourself stay.

Sometimes we have to do the
Hard things without applause,
Without recognition,

We have to give ourselves
The push, and the permission.

Pain is not a competition,
There are no winners when
It comes to suffering,

We're all in this together,
In growing and in recovering.

Don't seek worth
In other people,
Search for it inside,

No one else can tell
You to love yourself,
It's something you
Have to find.

Your pain does not
Diminish your strength,
It does not own the
Light you bring alive,

The dusk must
Bend to the dawn,
The sun will rise
Despite the night.

"Am I sick enough?"
Is a question born of
Our shame—that dark
Beast sitting heavy in
Our head,

Tell yourself we
All deserve help,
We all deserve
Better instead,

Let live your courage,
Let live your best intentions,
Until your worth is not
A truth that you feel
You have to question.

One day, maybe one day,
Your story will be the light
Guiding another on their
Path,

You—inspiring,
Even now in doing your best,
Precisely where you're at.

You have gifts no one
Else can express,
Don't let shame tell you that
Your talents are less.

Notice what's not working,
Reflect on that which improves,
Knowing what contributes
To a better day
Helps to decide what
To keep or to remove.

Your experience is valid,
Even if you've been told
Your feelings are wrong,

Your story has been
Worth hearing and
Telling all along.

Productivity is not
Validation of your worth,
Your worth is innate,
A given,

Do not feel
Guilt for resting,
For being, for living.

Do not assume the
Feelings of others,
The thoughts that
Aren't yours to think,
Desires or intentions,

We don't know what
Another is going through
If we don't ask,
Let your assumptions
Be questioned.

I've dreaded the future,
Thinking I couldn't be in it,
Thinking 'I'll be dead by then',

My death not an 'if' but a 'when',

It's a lonely place to be,
Convinced there's no bright
Light around the bend,
But I was wrong all along—
The clouds do pass,
The night does end,

And I wouldn't know it
If I wasn't still here now,
I wouldn't know it if I had
Listened to my doubt.

Challenge the worst
Your mind has to give,
Question, change, forgive,

There is more to you than
Your hurt, than your wounds,
The aching, the breaking,
Comes with healing, too.

What is true and
What is not,
When fear is
Taking the lead?

Sometimes the lies
That keep you small
Are easier to believe.

Another's kindness can challenge
How we've treated ourselves,
Can guide us to softer actions and words,

Self-compassion, self-love,
Is a practice we all can come to learn.

This is hard,
This getting better,
This becoming,
This path into
The unknown,

Don't fault yourself
For the struggle it
Takes to grow.

When it feels right,
Tell others your story,
The fight that you've
Been living every day,

You may help others feel seen,
Break down the stigma,
Knowing that others
Have lived the same way.

Your efforts aren't
Too small,
You are trying,
And that's what
Matters most of all.

You belong,
You will find
People that get you,
Things you love to do,
A place in the world,

Even if you feel
Like an outsider,
Home is something
You deserve.

Give it time,
Let it arrive,
Keep the hope
That hope is
A lightness you
Will find,

And when it does,
When it comes,
Don't be discouraged
When it leaves,

Trust that it will
Return again,
Be ready to receive.

Take shelter,
Take rest,
In the warm
Knowledge that
You're doing
Your best.

If I'd never made it today,
I never would have known—
Just how much I've always
Had the capacity to grow.

Cold hands,
Watch how the nail
Beds turn blue,
How strange to
To think that
That was me—
All quiet and sad
And alone,

Now I let the sunlight in,
Hands holding steady, warm,
A home.

Shift, rework,
Lungs full with
Each new breath,

Change comes in moments,
And at times change is
All that we have left,

Let it bring what it may,
Let it pass through
You as it lives,

Let yourself accept
The challenge, and the
Opportunities it can give.

Tossing, turning,
Awake when everything
Else is quiet, at rest,

When we feel we're
The last person awake,
That we're the only
Ones left,

Remember that
You are not alone,
There are others who
Feel the way that
You do,

Even in this night,
This dark, you can
See it through.

Sometimes our intentions don't align,
The lives we want do not connect,
It's up to you to decide between
Fulfillment and regret.

You don't have to
Have it all figured out,
You are whole as you are,
Even when there's so
Much more to become,
So much more to know,

A beautiful
Contradiction—
You are complete,
And you can grow.

P.Bodi

There is rhythm
To the world,
And there is a
Part made just
For you to play—
The harmony of you,

Full of all that
Only you can do.

You are not a let-down,
Not a burden for
Others to bear,

You deserve to be
Surrounded by those
Who fully love,
Who fully care.

Sanctuary, safety,
Hope shining bright
Despite what darkness
There may be around,

You have that lightness in you,
That steady fire to be found.

Count them, name them,
Claim them—all that you
Have to be proud of,

No effort is too small,
With each moment we
Are one step closer to
The person we want
To become.

Confidence can feel foreign,
A strange and stunning relief,

We always have room
To grow our self-belief.

There are mysteries in life,
But I know some
Things to be certain,

That you are worthy,
That you are enough,
That you have it in
You to make purpose.

Self-destruction, self-violence,
Self-sabotage that prefers our silence,

How to break the cycle,
The old ways of coping,
The downward spiral?

But this is not the end,
This is a slip, not a
Promise things will
Always be the same,

We can shift, grow,
Try again, rise above
Our shame.

Self-love is not a destination,
It is habit, a life long
Work-in-progress
That only you can do,

It a choice you have to
Make for you.

Your dreams matter,
They deserve your
Attention and
Your respect,

What is more painful:
Reaching or regret?

You are needed,
You belong,
The voices saying
Otherwise are wrong.

Listen to the way
Excitement can sound—
That's you, bright,
In bold, in color,

There is so much more of you,
And of your life, to discover.

Beauty is the least of you,
Look inside instead,
What qualities transcend
The surface?

What does it mean for
You to truly flourish?

Don't convince yourself that
You are the exception,
The dark cloud that
Blinds the sun forever,

I have thought myself the same,
But there's no truth in 'never',

Give yourself the chance
That only you can gift,
The space, the time, the hope
That these heavy skies will lift.

Your suffering is real,
It doesn't matter if
Someone else seems
To have it 'worse',

This is not a
Competition,
You are valid in
Your hurt.

Surround yourself with
Kindness, from others
As well as you, you may
Be surprised by the
Difference it makes,

Challenge the negative
Voices—there is a new
Narrative to create.

The night can feel heavier
Than the lightness of the day,
The sun's shine deemed
Irrelevant,

But it is a disservice to
Yourself to fall to
Pessimism,

Question the desire
To stay in the dark,
Every fresh dawn
Can be a new start.

Fear doesn't always make sense,
And even then, we listen to it,
Convinced that the worst
Is yet to come,

But we can choose not to
Believe what it has to say,
We can tell a different story,
We can overcome.

Don't assume that
Which you can change,
You are not fated for
A life of endless pain,

Expecting the worst
Ignores your capacity
For growth—endless,
Innate,

You are not at a dead-end,
And it is not too late.

If you are making
Any sort of change,
If you are changing,
If you are trying to
Change but don't
Feel different,

Keep going,
Keep growing,
You are stepping into
A life worth living.

Wake up to find
The morning
Exactly as it comes,

Never seen nor felt
Before, risen with
The new day's sun,

We rise just the same,
In this world of small
Beginnings,

Where rebirth is
Another name
For living.

Loneliness, disconnection,
Silence and shame,

A closed and quiet
Sort of pain,

I've been there too,
The only voice to hear
My own—harsh, cruel,
And unforgiving,

Being kind to myself first
Was the beginning.

What feels hopeless
Can be used—a flame
To light the fuse,

Sometimes our darkest
Moments can bring
The brightest change,

There lives endless
Opportunity in our
Deepest pain.

You are not here
To be entertaining,
Anxiety can tell us
We're boring,
Uninteresting,
Better off
Alone,

But that pressure is
A fiction, not a truth
You have to be living,
Your life is not
A show.

You've fought so
Hard every day,
Don't discount
Your efforts,
Even if they don't
Feel 'enough',

You are doing the best
You can to rise above.

P.Bodi

Believe it or don't,
You are worth a
Good life, friends,
And hope,

To be treated well,
And I think you'll
Come to see it too—

There is light,
A future, a place
Here for you.

You have two choices:
Stay the same or try to change,
You have to decide what type
Of pain you're willing to take,

While recovery may come with hope,
It also comes with being afraid,

But this fight is worth it,
And so are you,
Struggling and becoming
And pushing through.

Beliefs are hard to shift,
The ones that sit heavy
In your chest,

The ones that make
You think you're
Somehow less,

But they're wrong—
Nothing more,
You have been
Worthy all along,
Worthy to your core.

We are not fortune tellers,
Not prophets, our predictions
Are just that—not fact,

You have it in you:
To challenge that
Which feels true.

For those of us who are
Silent about pushing
Back against the dark,
With no recognition
And no applause ready
In reaching towards
The light,

You deserve to be proud
Of yourself, even if no
One else sees the
Battle you fight.

You are here still,
Despite it all,
Despite depression's
Siren call,

Be proud of
Your persistence,
Your presence,
Your perseverance,

There is strength
Within you,
There is resilience.

P.Bodi

Look at you,
Still here after
Everything—after
The worst you've
Ever felt, after the
Worst moments of
Your life,

You are growing,
You are glowing,
'Despite'.

You are not meant to
Be small—mute, withdrawn,
Caught in fear and self-hate,

There is hope for you yet,
It is patient, it waits.

Mourn your past,
It is a loss—
To lose old
Ways of being,
Of coping,
Of facing the
World and the
Pain it gives,

But there is another side now,
Another way to be, let it take
Its time to take root—
A softer life to live.

You can be a light for others,
That bright thing that shines
In the face of despair,

One day, healing might be
Something you can come
To share.

Shadows like to pull
And twist, and discount
What progress you've made,

Don't let them,
And don't forget
All the courage
That recovery takes.

Hold them close,
The dreams that
Keep you going,
Don't let anyone else
Take away the seeds
That you are growing.

You deserve better
From others,
Especially from
Yourself when it
Matters most,

You may slip,
You may fall,
And you may
Even lose hope,

And even then,
And even then,
We can trust it
Will return again.

We are all reaching out
Into the unknown,
Fingers spread
Against the night,

Eager to become
And to grow,
To touch the
Steady glow
Of daylight.

Not good enough for what?
For who? What is 'Good
Enough' to you?

Your worth cannot be
Measured, it's been in
You from the beginning,

Nothing could take your
Worth away, you are worthy
By virtue of living.

Every day you've lived,
You've survived to see
The next,

On hard days
To come,
Don't let your
Strength be a truth
That you forget.

I see you hiding there,
Face lost in the crowd,
But you are yourself,
No one better to be,

Repeat to yourself,
'This is me',
'This is me',
'This is me'.

There are people
You have yet to meet,
The kind of people
That want to lift you up,
Higher and higher, fly,

The kind that want to
See you touch the sky.

You are a bright thing,
A light in the dark,
This is a given:
You are human,

We all have the capacity
For growth, for a good life,
And for improvement.

It is not too late
For your dreams,
Your goals,
The person you
Want to become,

You are worth
That future, and
Change is never done.

We must make meaning,
We must make purpose,
It is a gift we can give
To ourselves and
Those around,

The most painful things
Can also be the most
Profound.

Self-forgiveness is a kindness,
A soft place to rest,
Whatever dark thing is in your past—
It doesn't make you less.

You've planted all the seeds,
You've opened to the sun,
You are ready to grow,
And you've only just begun.

This is an unknown,
Getting better,
Moving into
The dark—

So let your eyes adjust.

Our capacity for change
At times is something we
Just have to trust.

Maybe you didn't think
You'd still be alive by today,
Maybe you never thought
You'd make it one more day,

Let that be a gift,
Let yourself stay.

Your Story Continues

Thank you for giving this collection your time. It is written for your hope, it is written for your strength. In this moment, you are here, growing into that great unknown that is the rest of your life.

If these poems have helped you feel seen, heard, understood, or have provided a sense of hope, you can find more of my writing on Instagram @p.bodii. If you feel called to, you can share this book with others who may need to read these words.

Let this collection be a soft place for you to rest, let yourself come back as needed, and be reminded that you have recovery in you. It is patient, it waits.

Printed in Great Britain
by Amazon